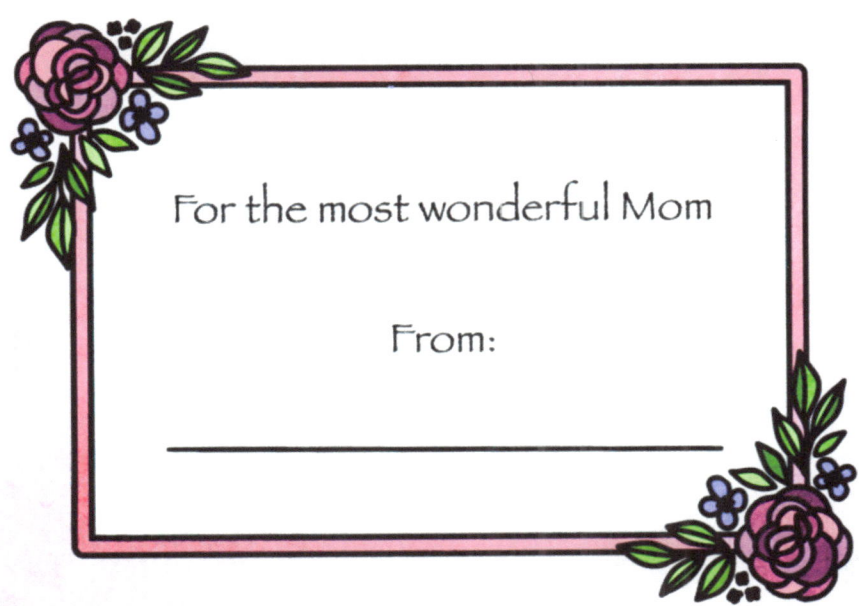

For the most wonderful Mom

From:

_____

Dear Mom,
I want to write to you
And tell you how much I love you.

I find comfort in your arms.
You keep me safe from any harm.

I love you more than words can say,
And I'll love you more with every day.

You teach me manners and how to share,
And show me how much you truly care.

I love it when we bake and cook,
And read stories from our favorite books.

You make the characters come alive,
And we share in the adventure, side by side.

You help me learn and grow each day,
And teach me to be kind in every way.

You pack my lunch each day for school,
And remind me to follow the golden rule.

You show me how to try new things
And are my strength, no matter what life brings.

You whisper words of love and care,
And I know you'll always be there.

I love the way you sing to me,
And help me fall asleep so peacefully.

You teach me how to be kind,
And to always keep an open mind.

When I'm feeling scared or sad,
You're the one who makes me glad.

When the day's hard, you're always near,
With a comforting smile and a listening ear.

You help me with my homework too,
And teach me things I never knew.

So thank you, Mom, for all you do,
And for always seeing me through.

I love you Mom.

Love always,
Your little one

For my mother

Discover more
great books

https://www.llgray.com

www.ingramcontent.com/pod-product-compliance
Lightning Source LLC
Chambersburg PA
CBHW041459120626
46547CB00003B/482